Kentucky
Planning Guide

for Scott Foresman Social Studies and the Kentucky Core Content for Assessment

D1072330

Contents

Editorial Offices: Glenview, Illinois • Parsippany, New Jersey
New York, New York
Sales Offices: Boston, Massachusetts • Duluth, Georgia • Glenview, Illinois
Coppell, Texas • Sacramento, California • Mesa, Arizona
www.sfsocialstudies.com

ISBN: 0-328-27186-1

1 2 3 4 5 6 7 8 9 10 V034 15 14 13 12 11 10 09 08 07 06

Kentucky Planning Guide

Unit 1 • Time for School

Begin with a Song pp. 2–3   **Vocabulary Preview** pp. 4–5

Lesson Titles	Pacing	Kentucky Core Content for Assessment
Lesson 1 Getting to Know Andrew pp. 8–9	2 days	*SS-EP-2.2.1 Students will identify social institutions and explain how they help the community.* (Also **SS-EP-2.3.1**)
Biography: Carl Stotz pp. 10–11		SS-EP-2.3.1 Students will describe various forms of interactions that occur between individuals/groups at home and at school. DOK 2 (Also **SS-EP-2.2.1, SS-EP-4.1.1, SS-EP-5.1.1**)
Colonial Williamsburg: Families Long Ago pp. 12–13		*SS-EP-5.1.1 Students will use a variety of primary and secondary sources to interpret the past.* (Also **SS-EP-2.1.1, SS-EP-2.2.1, SS-EP-2.3.1, SS-EP-4.3.2, SS-EP-4.4.1**)
Lesson 2 Home and School pp. 14–17	3 days	SS-EP-5.2.1 Students will identify significant patriotic and historical songs, symbols, monuments/landmarks, and patriotic holidays and explain their historical significance. DOK 2 (Also **SS-EP-2.1.1**, *SS-EP-2.2.1*, **SS-EP-2.3.1**)
★ **Citizen Heroes: Courage Ruby Bridges Hall** pp. 18–19		*SS-EP-5.2.3 Students will describe change over time in communication, technology, transportation, and education in the community.* (Also *SS-EP-2.1.2*, **SS-EP-2.2.1, SS-EP-2.3.1, SS-EP-4.1.1**)
Chart and Graph Skills: Read a Calendar pp. 20–21		SS-EP-2.1.1 Students will describe cultural elements. DOK 1 (Also **SS-EP-5.2.1**)
Lesson 3 Rules We Follow pp. 22–25	2 days	SS-EP-1.1.2 Students will identify and explain the purpose of rules within organizations and compare rules with laws. DOK 2 (Also **SS-EP-1.3.2**, *SS-EP-2.2.1*, **SS-EP-2.3.1**)
Thinking Skills: Problem on the Playground pp. 26–27		SS-EP-1.3.2 Students will identify and give examples of good citizenship at home, at school, and in the community and explain why civic engagement is important. DOK 2 (Also **SS-EP-2.3.1**)
Lesson 4 Learning About My School pp. 28–31	3 days	*SS-EP-5.2.3 Students will describe change over time in communication, technology, transportation, and education in the community.* (Also **SS-EP-2.2.1, SS-EP-5.1.1**)
Biography: Mary McLeod Bethune pp. 32–33		SS-EP-2.3.1 Students will describe various forms of interactions that occur between individuals/groups at home and at school. DOK 2 (Also **SS-EP-2.2.1, SS-EP-4.1.1, SS-EP-5.1.1, SS-EP-5.2.3**)
Then and Now: Things We Use pp. 34–35		*SS-EP-5.1.1 Students will use a variety of tools to learn about the past.* (Also **SS-EP-5.2.3**)

✔ **End with a Poem** pp. 36–37   ✔ **Unit 1 Review** pp. 38–41   ✔ **Unit 1 Project** p. 42   ✔ = Assessment Options

Target Skill

Reading Social Studies:
Use Picture Clues
pp. 6-7

Vocabulary	Resources	Meeting Individual Needs
school group	• Workbook, pp. 3-4 • Vocabulary Cards: school, group • Every Student Learns Guide, pp. 2-5	• Leveled Practice, TE p. 13a
flag country	• Workbook, pp. 5-6 • Vocabulary Cards: flag, country • Every Student Learns Guide, pp. 6-9 • Transparency 10	• ESL Support, TE p. 15 • Leveled Practice, TE pp. 16, 21a
rule	• Workbook, pp. 7-8 • Vocabulary Card: rule • Every Student Learns Guide, pp. 10-13 • Transparencies 11, 12	• ESL Support, TE p. 23 • Leveled Practice, TE p. 27a
	• Workbook, p. 9 • Every Student Learns Guide, pp. 14-17	• ESL Support, TE p. 29 • Learning Styles, TE p. 30 • Leveled Practice, TE pp. 35, 35a

Providing More Depth

Additional Resources

• Trade Books
• Family Activities
• Vocabulary Workbook and Cards
• Social Studies Plus!
• Daily Activity Bank
• Read Alouds and Primary Sources
• Big Book Atlas
• Primary Atlas
• Outline Maps
• Desk Maps

ADDITIONAL Technology

• Video Field Trips
• Songs and Music
• Digital Learning CD-ROM Powered by KnowledgeBox®
• AudioText
• MindPoint® Quiz Show CD-ROM
• ExamView® Test Bank CD-ROM
• Colonial Williamsburg Primary Sources CD-ROM
• Teacher Resources CD-ROM
• Map Resources CD-ROM
• SFSuccessNet: Online Student Edition, Online Teacher Edition, Online Planner
• www.sfsocialstudies.com (Biographies, news, references, maps, and activities)

⚠ To establish guidelines for children's safe and responsible use of the Internet, use the **Scott Foresman Internet Guide.**

Additional Internet Link
• Colonial Williamsburg, www.history.org

 ### Kentucky Core Content Test Prep

• Lesson 1, pp. 1-2
• Lesson 2, pp. 3-4
• Lesson 3, pp. 5-6
• Lesson 4, pp. 7-8

Unit 2 • In My Community

Begin with a Song pp. 44–45 **Vocabulary Preview** pp. 46–47

Lesson Titles	Pacing	Kentucky Core Content for Assessment
Lesson 1 Welcome to My Neighborhood pp. 50–53	2 days	*SS-EP-4.3.1* Students will describe patterns of human settlement in places and regions on the Earth's surface. (Also **SS-EP-2.3.1, SS-EP-4.1.1, SS-EP-4.1.2, SS-EP-4.4.1**)
Map and Globe Skills: Use a Map Key pp. 54–55		*SS-EP-4.1.1* Students will use geographic tools to locate and describe familiar places at home, at school, and in the community. (Also *SS-EP-4.1.2*)
Lesson 2 Different Kinds of Communities pp. 56–57	2 days	*SS-EP-4.3.2* Students will describe how technology helps us move, settle, and interact in the modern world. (Also *SS-EP-4.3.1*, **SS-EP-4.4.1, SS-EP-5.2.3**)
Then and Now: How a Community Changed pp. 58–59		*SS-EP-4.4.1* Students will describe ways people adapt to/modify the physical environment to meet their basic needs. DOK 1 (Also *SS-EP-4.3.1*, *SS-EP-4.4.2*, *SS-EP-5.1.1*, *SS-EP-5.2.3*)
Map and Globe Skills: Use Four Directions pp. 60–61		*SS-EP-4.1.1* Students will use geographic tools to locate and describe familiar places at home, at school, and in the community. (Also *SS-EP-4.1.2*)
Lesson 3 Special Things We Do pp. 62–65	3 days	SS-EP-2.3.1 Students will describe various forms of interactions that occur between individuals/groups at home and at school. DOK 2 (Also **SS-EP-2.1.1, SS-EP-2.1.2, SS-EP-2.2.1, SS-EP-5.2.1**)
[DK] **Chinese New Year** pp. 66–67		*SS-EP-2.1.2* Students will study a variety of diverse cultures locally and in the world today and explain the importance of appreciating and understanding other cultures (Also **SS-EP-2.1.1**)
⭐ **Citizen Heroes:** Fairness **Harriet Tubman** pp. 68–69		*SS-EP-2.3.2* Students will identify appropriate conflict resolution strategies. (Also **SS-EP-1.3.1, SS-EP-1.3.2, SS-EP-4.1.1**)
Lesson 4 Community Laws and Leaders pp. 70–71	2 days	*SS-EP-1.2.1* Students will describe how their local government is structured and compare their local government to other community governments in Kentucky. (Also **SS-EP-1.1.1, SS-EP-1.1.2, SS-EP-2.2.1, SS-EP-2.3.1**)
Biography: Jane Addams pp. 72–73		*SS-EP-5.1.1* Students will use a variety of primary and secondary sources to interpret the past. (Also **SS-EP-1.3.1, SS-EP-1.3.2, SS-EP-2.2.1, SS-EP-4.1.1**)
Lesson 5 Where in the World Do I Live? pp. 74–77	2 days	*SS-EP-4.2.1* Students will describe places on Earth's surface by their physical characteristics. (Also **SS-EP-4.1.1, SS-EP-4.1.2**)
Biography: Henry Flagler pp. 78–79		*SS-EP-4.3.2* Students will describe how technology helps us move, settle, and interact in the modern world. (Also **SS-EP-4.1.1, SS-EP-4.4.1, SS-EP-4.4.2, SS-EP-5.1.1**)

✔ **End with a Poem** pp. 80–81   ✔ **Unit 2 Review** pp. 82–85   ✔ **Unit 2 Project** p. 86   ✔ = Assessment Options

Target Skill

Reading Social Studies:
Alike and Different
pp. 48–49

Vocabulary	Resources	Meeting Individual Needs
neighborhood	• Workbook, pp. 14–15 • Vocabulary Card: neighborhood • Every Student Learns Guide, pp. 18–21 • Transparencies 13, 14	• ESL Support, TE p. 52 • Leveled Practice, TE p. 55a
community	• Workbook, pp. 16–17 • Vocabulary Card: community • Every Student Learns Guide, pp. 22–25 • Transparency 15	• ESL Support, TE pp. 58, 61 • Leveled Practice, TE p. 61a
	• Workbook, p. 18 • Every Student Learns Guide, pp. 26–29	• ESL Support, TE p. 64 • Leveled Practice, TE p. 69a
law leader	• Workbook, p. 19 • Vocabulary Cards: law, leader • Every Student Learns Guide, pp. 30–33	• Leveled Practice, TE pp. 73, 73a
state continent ocean	• Workbook, p. 20 • Vocabulary Cards: state, continent, ocean • Every Student Learns Guide, pp. 34–37 • Transparencies 16, 17	• ESL Support, TE p. 76 • Leveled Practice, TE p. 79a

Providing More Depth

Additional Resources

• Trade Books
• Family Activities
• Vocabulary Workbook and Cards
• Social Studies Plus!
• Daily Activity Bank
• Read Alouds and Primary Sources
• Big Book Atlas
• Primary Atlas
• Outline Maps
• Desk Maps

ADDITIONAL Technology

• Video Field Trips
• Songs and Music
• Digital Learning CD-ROM Powered by KnowledgeBox®
• AudioText
• MindPoint® Quiz Show CD-ROM
• ExamView® Test Bank CD-ROM
• Colonial Williamsburg Primary Sources CD-ROM
• Teacher Resources CD-ROM
• Map Resources CD-ROM
• SFSuccessNet: Online Student Edition, Online Teacher Edition, Online Planner
• **www.sfsocialstudies.com** (Biographies, news, references, maps, and activities)

⚠ To establish guidelines for children's safe and responsible use of the Internet, use the **Scott Foresman Internet Guide.**

Additional Internet Links

• Visit the Web site for your village, town, or city.
• Henry Flagler, **www.flaglermuseum.us**

 ## Kentucky Core Content Test Prep

• Lesson 1, pp. 9–10
• Lesson 2, pp. 11–12
• Lesson 3, pp. 13–14
• Lesson 4, pp. 15–16
• Lesson 5, pp. 17–18

Kentucky Planning Guide

Unit 3 • Work! Work! Work!

Begin with a Song pp. 88–89 **Vocabulary Preview** pp. 90–91

Lesson Titles	Pacing	Kentucky Core Content for Assessment
Lesson 1 Ben's Jobs pp. 94–97	2 days	*SS-EP-2.2.1* Students will identify social institutions and explain how they help the community. (Also **SS-EP-2.3.1**, **SS-EP-3.4.3**)
Chart and Graph Skills: Use a Chart pp. 98–99		**SS-EP-2.3.1** Students will describe various forms of interactions that occur between individuals/groups at home and at school. DOK 2 (Also **SS-EP-3.4.3**)
Lesson 2 Needs and Wants pp. 100–101	2 days	*SS-EP-3.3.2* Students will explain different ways that people acquire goods and services. (Also **SS-EP-2.2.1**, **SS-EP-3.1.1**)
Then and Now: Changing Toys pp. 102–103		*SS-EP-5.1.1* Students will use a variety of primary and secondary sources to interpret the past.
Lesson 3 Spending and Saving pp. 104–105	2 days	**SS-EP-3.1.1** Students will define basic economic terms related to scarcity and explain that scarcity requires people to make economic choices and incur opportunity costs. DOK 2 (Also **SS-EP-2.2.1**, **SS-EP-3.2.1**, **SS-EP-3.3.1**)
Here and There: Money Around the World pp. 106–107		*SS-EP-3.3.2* Students will explain different ways that people acquire goods and services. (Also **SS-EP-2.1.1**, **SS-EP-3.2.1**, **SS-EP-3.3.1**, **SS-EP-3.4.1**)
Lesson 4 Welcome to Job Day! pp. 108–111	3 days	**SS-EP-3.3.1** Students will define basic economic terms related to markets. DOK 2 (Also **SS-EP-2.2.1**, **SS-EP-3.4.1**, **SS-EP-3.4.2**, **SS-EP-3.4.3**)
⭐ **Citizen Heroes:** Caring **Kid's Kitchen** pp. 112–113		**SS-EP-1.3.2** Students will identify and give examples of good citizenship at home, at school, and in the community and explain why civic engagement is important. DOK 2 (Also **SS-EP-2.3.1**, **SS-EP-3.1.1**, **SS-EP-4.1.1**)
Biography: Clara Barton pp. 114-115		*SS-EP-5.1.1* Students will use a variety of primary and secondary sources to interpret the past. (Also **SS-EP-1.3.2**, **SS-EP-4.1.1**)
Lesson 5 Interview with a Farmer pp. 116–119	3 days	**SS-EP-3.4.1** Students will define basic economic terms related to production, distribution, and consumption and describe various ways goods and services are distributed. DOK 2 (Also **SS-EP-2.2.1**, **SS-EP-3.4.2**, **SS-EP-3.4.3**, **SS-EP-4.4.1**)
Map and Globe Skills: Follow a Route pp. 120–121		*SS-EP-4.1.1* Students will use geographic tools to locate and describe familiar places at home, at school, and in the community. (Also **SS-EP-4.1.2**)
Biography: George Washington Carver pp. 122–123		*SS-EP-3.4.2* Students will describe how new knowledge, technology/tools, and specialization increases productivity in our community, state, nation, and world. (Also **SS-EP-4.1.1**, **SS-EP-4.4.1**, **SS-EP-5.1.1**)
Lesson 6 From Place to Place pp. 124–125	2 days	*SS-EP-3.4.2* Students will describe how new knowledge, technology/tools, and specialization increases productivity in our community, state, nation, and world. (Also **SS-EP-3.4.1**, **SS-EP-4.3.2**, **SS-EP-5.2.3**)
DK Transportation pp. 126–127		*SS-EP-4.3.2* Students will describe how technology helps us move, settle, and interact in the modern world. (Also **SS-EP-3.4.1**, **SS-EP-5.2.3**)

✔ **End with a Poem** pp. 128–129 ✔ **Unit 3 Review** pp. 130–133 ✔ **Unit 3 Project** p. 134 ✔ = Assessment Options

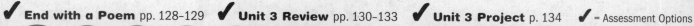

Reading Social Studies:
Sequence
pp. 92–93

Vocabulary	Resources	Meeting Individual Needs
job	• Workbook, pp. 25–26 • Transparencies 9, 19 • Vocabulary Card: job • Every Student Learns Guide, pp. 38–41	• ESL Support, TE p. 96 • Leveled Practice, TE p. 99a
needs wants	• Workbook, p. 27 • Vocabulary Cards: needs, wants • Every Student Learns Guide, pp. 42–45	• ESL Support, TE p. 101 • Leveled Practice, TE p. 103a
	• Workbook, p. 28 • Every Student Learns Guide, pp. 46–49 • Transparency 20	• ESL Support, TE p. 105 • Leveled Practice, TE p. 107a
tools goods service volunteer	• Workbook, p. 29 • Vocabulary Cards: tools, goods, service, volunteer • Every Student Learns Guide, pp. 50–53	• ESL Support, TE p. 110 • Leveled Practice, TE p. 115a
	• Workbook, pp. 30–31 • Transparencies 9, 21 • Every Student Learns Guide, pp. 54–57	• ESL Support, TE p. 118 • Leveled Practice, TE p. 123a
transportation	• Workbook, p. 32 • Vocabulary Card: transportation • Every Student Learns Guide, pp. 58–61	• ESL Support, TE p. 126 • Leveled Practice, TE p. 127a

Providing More Depth

Additional Resources
- Trade Books
- Family Activities
- Vocabulary Workbook and Cards
- Social Studies Plus!
- Daily Activity Bank
- Read Alouds and Primary Sources
- Big Book Atlas
- Primary Atlas
- Outline Maps
- Desk Maps

ADDITIONAL Technology

- Video Field Trips
- Songs and Music
- Digital Learning CD-ROM Powered by KnowledgeBox®
- AudioText
- MindPoint® Quiz Show CD-ROM
- ExamView® Test Bank CD-ROM
- Colonial Williamsburg Primary Sources CD-ROM
- Teacher Resources CD-ROM
- Map Resources CD-ROM
- SFSuccessNet: Online Student Edition, Online Teacher Edition, Online Planner
- **www.sfsocialstudies.com** (Biographies, news, references, maps, and activities)

 To establish guidelines for children's safe and responsible use of the Internet, use the **Scott Foresman Internet Guide.**

Additional Internet Links
- Being a smart consumer, **www.zillions.org**.
- Trains, California State Railroad, **www.csrmf.org**

 ### Kentucky Core Content Test Prep

- Lesson 1, pp. 19–20
- Lesson 2, pp. 21–22
- Lesson 3, pp. 23–24
- Lesson 4, pp. 25–26
- Lesson 5, pp. 27–28
- Lesson 6, pp. 29–30

Unit 4 • Our Earth, Our Resources

Begin with a Song pp. 136–137 **Vocabulary Preview** pp. 138–139

Lesson Titles	Pacing	Kentucky Core Content for Assessment
Lesson 1 **Different Kinds of Weather** pp. 142–145		**SS-EP-4.4.2** *Students will describe how the physical environment can both promote and restrict human activities.* (Also **SS-EP-4.1.1**)
Chart and Graph Skills: Read a Time Line pp. 146–147	2 days	**SS-EP-5.1.1** *Students will use a variety of primary and secondary sources to interpret the past.* (Also **SS-EP-4.4.2**)
Colonial Williamsburg: Weather and Seasons Long Ago pp. 148–149		**SS-EP-4.4.1** Students will describe ways people adapt to/modify the physical environment to meet their basic needs. DOK 1 (Also **SS-EP-2.2.1, SS-EP-4.4.2, SS-EP-5.1.1, SS-EP-5.2.3**)
Lesson 2 **Looking at Our Land and Water** pp. 150–153		**SS-EP-4.2.1** *Students will describe places on Earth's surface by their physical characteristics.* (Also **SS-EP-4.1.3, SS-EP-4.4.2**)
Map and Globe Skills: Locate Land and Water pp. 154–155	2 days	**SS-EP-4.1.1** *Students will use geographic tools to locate and describe familiar places at home, at school, and in the community.* (Also **SS-EP-4.1.2, SS-EP-4.2.1**)
Lesson 3 **Our Earth's Resources** pp. 156–159		**SS-EP-4.1.3** *Students will describe how different factors influence where human activities are located in the community.* (Also **SS-EP-1.3.2, SS-EP-3.1.1, SS-EP-4.3.2, SS-EP-4.4.1**)
Citizen Heroes: (Responsibility) Tree Musketeers pp. 160–161	3 days	**SS-EP-1.3.2** Students will identify and give examples of good citizenship at home, at school, and in the community and explain why civic engagement is important. DOK 2 (Also **SS-EP-2.3.1, SS-EP-4.1.1**)
Biography: Elvia Niebla pp. 162–163		**SS-EP-1.1.2** Students will identify and explain the purpose of rules within organizations and compare rules with laws. DOK 2 (Also **SS-EP-1.3.2, SS-EP-4.1.1, SS-EP-5.1.1**)
Lesson 4 **Interview About Farm History** pp. 164–167		**SS-EP-4.3.1** *Students will describe patterns of human settlement in places and regions on the Earth's surface.* (Also **SS-EP-4.4.1, SS-EP-5.1.1, SS-EP-5.2.2, SS-EP-5.2.3**)
Biography: Sacagawea pp. 168–169	2 days	**SS-EP-2.3.1** *Students will describe various forms of interactions that occur between individuals/groups at home and at school. DOK 2* (Also **SS-EP-2.1.1, SS-EP-4.1.1, SS-EP-5.1.1**)
Lesson 5 **Caring for Our Resources** pp. 170–173		**SS-EP-1.3.2** Students will identify and give examples of good citizenship at home, at school, and in the community and explain why civic engagement is important. DOK 2 (Also **SS-EP-2.3.1**)
Here and There: Endangered Animals pp. 174–175	2 days	**SS-EP-4.1.2** *Students will use geographic tools to identify major landforms, bodies of water, and natural resources on Earth's surface and use relative location.* (Also **SS-EP-1.1.1, SS-EP-2.2.1**)

✔ **End with a Legend** pp. 176–177   ✔ **Unit 4 Review** pp. 178–181   ✔ **Unit 4 Project** p. 182   ✔ = Assessment Option

Target Skill

Reading Social Studies:
Find the Main Idea
pp. 140–141

Vocabulary	Resources	Meeting Individual Needs
weather	• Workbook, pp. 37–39 • Vocabulary Card: weather • Every Student Learns Guide, pp. 62–65 • Transparency 22	• ESL Support, TE p. 144 • Leveled Practice, TE p. 149a
mountain plain lake river	• Workbook, pp. 40–41 • Vocabulary Cards: mountain, plain, lake, river • Every Student Learns Guide, pp. 66–69 • Transparency 23	• ESL Support, TE pp. 151, 154 • Leveled Practice, TE p. 155a
natural resource	• Workbook, p. 42 • Vocabulary Card: natural resource • Every Student Learns Guide, pp. 70–73	• ESL Support, TE pp. 157, 162 • Leveled Practice, TE p. 163a
history	• Workbook, p. 43 • Vocabulary Card: history • Every Student Learns Guide, pp. 74–77	• ESL Support, TE p. 166 • Leveled Practice, TE p. 169a
	• Workbook, p. 44 • Every Student Learns Guide, pp. 78–81 • Transparency 24	• ESL Support, TE p. 171 • Leveled Practice, TE p. 175a

Providing More Depth

Additional Resources
• Trade Books
• Family Activities
• Vocabulary Workbook and Cards
• Social Studies Plus!
• Daily Activity Bank
• Read Alouds and Primary Sources
• Big Book Atlas
• Primary Atlas
• Outline Maps
• Desk Maps

ADDITIONAL Technology

• Video Field Trips
• Songs and Music
• Digital Learning CD-ROM Powered by KnowledgeBox®
• AudioText
• MindPoint® Quiz Show CD-ROM
• ExamView® Test Bank CD-ROM
• Colonial Williamsburg Primary Sources CD-ROM
• Teacher Resources CD-ROM
• Map Resources CD-ROM
• SFSuccessNet: Online Student Edition, Online Teacher Edition, Online Planner
• www.sfsocialstudies.com (Biographies, news, references, maps, and activities)

 To establish guidelines for children's safe and responsible use of the Internet, use the **Scott Foresman Internet Guide.**

Additional Internet Link
• Tree Musketeers, **Info@TreeMusketeers.org**
• Living History Farms, **www.lhf.org**

 ### Kentucky Core Content Test Prep

• Lesson 1, pp. 31–32
• Lesson 2, pp. 33–34
• Lesson 3, pp. 35–36
• Lesson 4, pp. 37–38
• Lesson 5, pp. 39–40

Kentucky Planning Guide

Unit 5 • This Is Our Country

Begin with a Song pp. 184–185   **Vocabulary Preview** pp. 186–187

Lesson Titles	Pacing	Kentucky Core Content for Assessment
Lesson 1 **Native Americans** pp. 190–191	3 days	**SS-EP-5.2.2** Students will identify and compare the early cultures of diverse groups of Native Americans and explain why they settled in what is now the United States. DOK 2 (Also *SS-EP-4.3.1*, SS-EP-4.4.1, *SS-EP-4.4.2*, *SS-EP-5.1.1*)
Chart and Graph Skills: Read a Diagram pp. 192–193		**SS-EP-4.4.1** Students will describe ways people adapt to/modify the physical environment to meet their basic needs. DOK 1 (Also *SS-EP-5.1.1*)
DK **Native American Objects** pp. 194–195		**SS-EP-2.1.1** Students will describe cultural elements. DOK 1 (Also *SS-EP-4.4.1*, *SS-EP-5.1.1*, *SS-EP-5.2.2*, *SS-EP-5.2.3*)
Lesson 2 **Early Travelers to America** pp. 196–199	2 days	*SS-EP-4.3.1 Students will describe patterns of human settlement in places and regions on the Earth's surface. (Also SS-EP-1.3.1, SS-EP-5.1.1, SS-EP-5.2.1)*
Map and Globe Skills: Use a History Map pp. 200–201		*SS-EP-4.1.2 Students will use geographic tools to identify major landforms, bodies of water, and natural resources on Earth's surface and use relative location. (Also SS-EP-4.3.1, SS-EP-5.1.1)*
Lesson 3 **The Colonies Become Free** pp. 202–205	2 days	**SS-EP-5.2.1** Students will identify significant patriotic and historical songs, symbols, monuments/landmarks, and patriotic holidays and explain their historical significance. DOK 2 (Also *SS-EP-1.3.1*, SS-EP-1.3.2, SS-EP-2.1.1, *SS-EP-5.1.1*)
Biography: Benjamin Franklin pp. 206–207		**SS-EP-1.3.2** Students will identify and give examples of good citizenship at home, at school, and in the community and explain why civic engagement is important. DOK 2 (Also *SS-EP-4.1.1*, SS-EP-5.1.1)
Lesson 4 **Symbols in Our Country** pp. 208–209	2 days	**SS-EP-5.2.1** Students will identify significant patriotic and historical songs, symbols, monuments/landmarks, and patriotic holidays and explain their historical significance. DOK 2 (Also *SS-EP-1.3.1*)
Then and Now: Our Country's Flag pp. 210–211		*SS-EP-5.1.1 Students will use a variety of primary and secondary sources to interpret the past. (Also SS-EP-2.1.2, SS-EP-5.2.1)*
Lesson 5 **We Celebrate Holidays** pp. 212–215	2 days	**SS-EP-2.1.1** Students will describe cultural elements. DOK 1 (Also *SS-EP-1.3.1*, SS-EP-1.3.2, *SS-EP-5.1.1*, SS-EP-5.2.1)
Biography: Abraham Lincoln pp. 216–217		*SS-EP-1.3.1 Students will define basic democratic ideas and explain why they are important today. (Also SS-EP-4.1.1, SS-EP-5.1.1, SS-EP-5.2.1)*
Lesson 6 **Choosing Our Country's Leaders** pp. 218–221	2 days	*SS-EP-2.2.1 Students will identify social institutions and explain how they help the community. (Also SS-EP-1.2.1, SS-EP-1.3.1, SS-EP-1.3.2, SS-EP-4.1.1)*
⭐ **Citizen Heroes:** Honesty **Eleanor Roosevelt** pp. 222–223		**SS-EP-1.3.2** Students will identify and give examples of good citizenship at home, at school, and in the community and explain why civic engagement is important. DOK 2 (Also *SS-EP-1.3.1*, SS-EP-4.1.1, *SS-EP-5.1.1*)

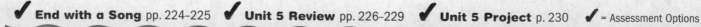

✔ **End with a Song** pp. 224–225   ✔ **Unit 5 Review** pp. 226–229   ✔ **Unit 5 Project** p. 230   ✔ = Assessment Options

Reading Social Studies:
Recall and Retell
pp. 188–189

Vocabulary	Resources	Meeting Individual Needs
	• Workbook, pp. 49–51 • Every Student Learns Guide, pp. 82–85 • Transparencies 25, 26	• ESL Support, TE p. 192 • Leveled Practice, TE p. 195a
freedom	• Workbook, pp. 52–53 • Vocabulary Card: freedom • Every Student Learns Guide, pp. 86–89 • Transparency 27	• ESL Support, TE p. 198 • Leveled Practice, TE p. 201a
colony	• Workbook, p. 54 • Vocabulary Card: colony • Every Student Learns Guide, pp. 90–93 • Transparency 28	• ESL Support, TE p. 204 • Leveled Practice, TE p. 207a
	• Workbook, p. 55 • Every Student Learns Guide, pp. 94–97 • Transparencies 29, 30	• ESL Support, TE p. 210 • Leveled Practice, TE p. 211a
holiday President	• Workbook, p. 56 • Vocabulary Cards: holiday, President • Every Student Learns Guide, pp. 98–101 • Transparencies 31, 32	• ESL Support, TE p. 214 • Leveled Practice, TE p. 217a
citizen vote capital	• Workbook, p. 57 • Vocabulary Cards: citizen, vote, capital • Every Student Learns Guide, pp. 102–105	• ESL Support, TE p. 220 • Leveled Practice, TE p. 223a

Providing More Depth

Additional Resources

- Trade Books
- Family Activities
- Vocabulary Workbook and Cards
- Social Studies Plus!
- Daily Activity Bank
- Read Alouds and Primary Sources
- Big Book Atlas
- Primary Atlas
- Outline Maps
- Desk Maps

 ### ADDITIONAL Technology

- Video Field Trips
- Songs and Music
- Digital Learning CD-ROM Powered by KnowledgeBox®
- AudioText
- MindPoint® Quiz Show CD-ROM
- ExamView® Test Bank CD-ROM
- Colonial Williamsburg Primary Sources CD-ROM
- Teacher Resources CD-ROM
- Map Resources CD-ROM
- SFSuccessNet: Online Student Edition, Online Teacher Edition, Online Planner
- **www.sfsocialstudies.com** (Biographies, news, references, maps, and activities)

 To establish guidelines for children's safe and responsible use of the Internet, use the **Scott Foresman Internet Guide.**

Additional Internet Link
- Pilgrims, **www.plimoth.org**

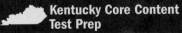 ### Kentucky Core Content Test Prep

- Lesson 1, pp. 41–42
- Lesson 2, pp. 43–44
- Lesson 3, pp. 45–46
- Lesson 4, pp. 47–48
- Lesson 5, pp. 49–50
- Lesson 6, pp. 51–52

Lesson Titles	Pacing	Kentucky Core Content for Assessment
Lesson 1 **Visiting the Market** pp. 238–239	2 days	*SS-EP-3.4.3* *Students will define interdependence and give examples of how people in our communities, states, nation, and world depend on each other for goods and services.* (Also **SS-EP-3.3.1**, **SS-EP-3.3.2**, **SS-EP-3.4.1**)
Gather Information pp. 240–241		*SS-EP-5.1.1* *Students will use a variety of primary and secondary sources to interpret the past.*
Lesson 2 **How Things Have Changed** pp. 242–243	2 days	*SS-EP-5.2.3* *Students will describe change over time in communication, technology, transportation, and education in the community.* (Also **SS-EP-2.2.1**, **SS-EP-4.3.2**, **SS-EP-5.1.1**)
⭐ **Citizen Heroes:** **Respect** **Joseph Bruchac** pp. 244–245		*SS-EP-2.1.1* *Students will describe cultural elements. DOK 1* (Also **SS-EP-1.3.2**, **SS-EP-4.1.1**)
Lesson 3 **Inventors and Inventions** pp. 246–249	2 days	*SS-EP-4.3.2* *Students will describe how technology helps us move, settle, and interact in the modern world.* (Also **SS-EP-2.1.1**, **SS-EP-5.1.1**, **SS-EP-5.2.3**)
📖 **Telephones** pp. 250–251		*SS-EP-5.1.1* *Students will use a variety of primary and secondary sources to interpret the past.* (Also **SS-EP-4.3.2**, **SS-EP-5.2.3**)
Lesson 4 **How Travel Has Changed** pp. 252–253	3 days	*SS-EP-5.2.3* *Students will describe change over time in communication, technology, transportation, and education in the community.* (Also **SS-EP-3.4.1**, **SS-EP-4.3.2**, **SS-EP-5.1.1**)
Chart and Graph Skills: Read a Bar Graph pp. 254–255		*SS-EP-4.3.2* *Students will describe how technology helps us move, settle, and interact in the modern world.*
Biography: Mae Jemison pp. 256–257		*SS-EP-1.3.1* *Students will define basic democratic ideas and explain why they are important today.* (Also **SS-EP-1.3.2**, **SS-EP-4.1.1**, **SS-EP-5.1.1**)
Lesson 5 **Life Around the World** pp. 258–261	3 days	*SS-EP-2.1.2* *Students will study a variety of diverse cultures locally and in the world today and explain the importance of appreciating and understanding other cultures.* (Also **SS-EP-2.1.1**, **SS-EP-4.1.2**, **SS-EP-4.4.1**)
Biography: Laurence Yep pp. 262–263		*SS-EP-2.1.1* *Students will describe cultural elements. DOK 1* (Also **SS-EP-4.1.1**, **SS-EP-4.3.1**, **SS-EP-5.1.1**)
Here and There: It Is Time to Leave pp. 264–265		*SS-EP-2.1.2* *Students will study a variety of diverse cultures locally and in the world today and explain the importance of appreciating and understanding other cultures.* (Also **SS-EP-4.1.2**)

✔ **End with a Folktale** pp. 266–267   ✔ **Unit 6 Review** pp. 268–271   ✔ **Unit 6 Project** p. 272   ✔ = Assessment Optic

Reading Social Studies:
Predict
pp. 236–237

Vocabulary	Resources	Meeting Individual Needs
market	• Workbook, pp. 62–63 • Vocabulary Card: market • Every Student Learns Guide, pp. 106–109 • Transparency 34	• ESL Support, TE p. 240 • Leveled Practice, TE p. 241a
	• Workbook, p. 64 • Every Student Learns Guide, pp. 110–113	• ESL Support, TE p. 243 • Leveled Practice, TE p. 245a
communicate invention inventor	• Workbook, p. 65 • Vocabulary Cards: communicate, invention, inventor • Every Student Learns Guide, pp. 114–117	• ESL Support, TE p. 248 • Leveled Practice, TE p. 251a
	• Workbook, pp. 66–67 • Every Student Learns Guide, pp. 118–121 • Transparency 35	• ESL Support, TE p. 257 • Leveled Practice, TE p. 257a
world	• Workbook, p. 68 • Vocabulary Card: world • Every Student Learns Guide, pp. 122–125 • Transparency 36	• ESL Support, TE p. 260 • Leveled Practice, TE p. 265a

Providing More Depth

Additional Resources

- Trade Books
- Family Activities
- Vocabulary Workbook and Cards
- Social Studies Plus!
- Daily Activity Bank
- Read Alouds and Primary Sources
- Big Book Atlas
- Primary Atlas
- Outline Maps
- Desk Maps

 ADDITIONAL Technology

- Video Field Trips
- Songs and Music
- Digital Learning CD-ROM Powered by KnowledgeBox®
- AudioText
- MindPoint® Quiz Show CD-ROM
- ExamView® Test Bank CD-ROM
- Colonial Williamsburg Primary Sources CD-ROM
- Teacher Resources CD-ROM
- Map Resources CD-ROM
- SFSuccessNet: Online Student Edition, Online Teacher Edition, Online Planner
- www.sfsocialstudies.com (Biographies, news, references, maps, and activities)

⚠ To establish guidelines for children's safe and responsible use of the Internet, use the **Scott Foresman Internet Guide.**

Additional Internet Link

- Views of space from Earth, **www.nasa.gov**
- Views of Earth from space, **http://earth.jsc.nasa.gov**

Kentucky Core Content Test Prep

- Lesson 1, pp. 53–54
- Lesson 2, pp. 55–56
- Lesson 3, pp. 57–58
- Lesson 4, pp. 59–60
- Lesson 5, pp. 61–62

GOVERNMENT AND CIVICS

Formation of Governments

SS-EP-1.1.1 Students will identify the basic purposes of local government (to establish order, provide security, and accomplish common goals), give examples of services local governments provide (e.g., police and fire protection, roads and snow removal, garbage pick-up), and identify how they pay for these services (taxes).

SS-EP-1.1.2 Students will identify and explain the purpose of rules within organizations (e.g., school, clubs, teams) and compare rules with laws. DOK 2

Constitutional Principles

SS-EP-1.2.1 Students will describe how their local government is structured (e.g., mayor, city council, judge-executive, fiscal court, local courts) and compare their local government to other community governments in Kentucky.

Rights and Responsibilities

SS-EP-1.3.1 Students will define basic democratic ideas (e.g., liberty, justice, equality, rights, responsibility) and explain why they are important today.

SS-EP-1.3.2 Students will identify and give examples of good citizenship at home, at school, and in the community (e.g., helping with chores, obeying rules, participating in community service projects such as recycling, conserving natural resources, donating food/supplies) and explain why civic engagement in the community is important. DOK 2

CULTURES AND SOCIETIES

Elements of Culture

SS-EP-2.1.1 Students will describe cultural elements (e.g., beliefs, traditions, languages, skills, literature, the arts). DOK 1

SS-EP-2.1.2 Students will study a variety of diverse cultures locally and in the world today

and explain the importance of appreciating and understanding other cultures.

Social Institutions

SS-EP-2.2.1 Students will identify social institutions (government, economy, education, religion, family) and explain how they help the community.

Interactions Among Individuals and Groups

SS-EP-2.3.1 Students will describe various forms of interactions (compromise, cooperation, conflict, competition) that occur between individuals/groups at home and at school. DOK 2

SS-EP-2.3.2 Students will identify appropriate conflict resolution strategies (e.g., compromise, cooperation, communication).

ECONOMICS

Scarcity

SS-EP-3.1.1 Students will define basic economic terms related to scarcity (e.g., opportunity cost, wants and needs, limited productive resources—natural, human, capital) and explain that scarcity requires people to make economic choices and incur opportunity costs. DOK 2

Economic Systems and Institutions

SS-EP-3.2.1 Students will identify and give examples of economic institutions (banks) and explain how they help people deal with the problem of scarcity (e.g., loan money, save money) in today's market economy.

Markets

SS-EP-3.3.1 Students will define basic economic terms related to markets (e.g., market economy, markets, wants and needs, goods and services, profit, consumer, producer, supply and demand, barter, money, trade, advertising). DOK 2

SS-EP-3.3.2 *Students will explain different ways that people acquire goods and services (by trading/bartering goods and services for other goods and services or by using money).*

Production, Distribution, and Consumption

SS-EP-3.4.1 Students will define basic economic terms related to production, distribution, and consumption (e.g., goods and services, wants and needs, supply and demand, specialization, entrepreneur) and describe various ways goods and services are distributed (e.g., by price, first-come-first-served, sharing equally). DOK 2

SS-EP-3.4.2 *Students will describe how new knowledge, technology/tools, and specialization increases productivity in our community, state, nation, and world.*

SS-EP-3.4.3 *Students will define interdependence and give examples of how people in our communities, states, nation, and world depend on each other for goods and services.*

GEOGRAPHY

The Use of Geographic Tools

SS-EP-4.1.1 *Students will use geographic tools (e.g., maps, globes, mental maps, charts, graphs) to locate and describe familiar places at home, at school, and in the community.*

SS-EP-4.1.2 *Students will use geographic tools to identify major landforms (e.g., continents, mountain ranges), bodies of water (e.g., oceans, major rivers), and natural resources on Earth's surface and use relative location.*

SS-EP-4.1.3 *Students will describe how different factors (e.g., rivers, mountains) influence where human activities are located in the community.*

Regions

SS-EP-4.2.1 *Students will describe places on Earth's surface by their physical characteristics (e.g., climate, landforms, bodies of water).*

Patterns

SS-EP-4.3.1 *Students will describe patterns of human settlement in places and regions on the Earth's surface.*

SS-EP-4.3.2 *Students will describe how technology helps us move, settle, and interact in the modern world.*

Human-Environment Interaction

SS-EP-4.4.1 Students will describe ways people adapt to/modify the physical environment to meet their basic needs (food, shelter, clothing). DOK 1

SS-EP-4.4.2 *Students will describe how the physical environment can both promote and restrict human activities.*

HISTORICAL PERSPECTIVE

The Factual and Interpretive Nature of History

SS-EP-5.1.1 *Students will use a variety of primary and secondary sources (e.g., artifacts, diaries, time lines) to interpret the past.*

The History of the United States

SS-EP-5.2.1 Students will identify significant patriotic and historical songs, symbols, monuments/landmarks (e.g., "The Star-Spangled Banner," the Underground Railroad, the Statue of Liberty), and patriotic holidays (e.g., Veterans day, Martin Luther King's birthday, Fourth of July) and explain their historical significance. DOK 2

SS-EP-5.2.2 Students will identify and compare the early cultures of diverse groups of Native Americans (e.g., Northwest, Southwest, Plains, Eastern Woodlands) and explain why they settled in what is now the United States. DOK 2

SS-EP-5.2.3 *Students will describe change over time in communication, technology, transportation, and education in the community.*